# CLIMATE CHANGE

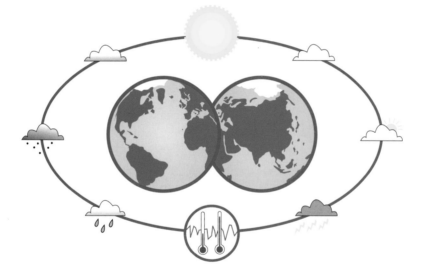

KINGFISHER
NEW YORK

## KINGFISHER
LONDON & NEW YORK

Text and design copyright © Toucan Books Ltd. 2014
Based on an original concept by Toucan Books Ltd.
Illustrations copyright © Simon Basher 2014

Published in the United States by Kingfisher,
175 Fifth Ave., New York, NY 10010
Kingfisher is an imprint of Macmillan Children's Books, London.

Consultants: Dr. John Fasullo, Dr. Jennifer Kay, Dr. Kirk Maasch
Expert reviewer for Chapters 1 and 2: Dr. Virginia Burkett

Designed and created by Basher
www.basherbooks.com
Text written by Dan Green

Dedicated to Chloe Ham

Distributed in the U.S. and Canada by Macmillan, 175 Fifth Ave., New York,
NY 10010

Library of Congress Cataloging-in-Publication Data
has been applied for

ISBN: 978-0-7534-7176-0 (HC)
ISBN: 978-0-7534-7175-3 (PB)

Kingfisher books are available for special promotions and premiums.
For details contact: Special Markets Department, Macmillan,
175 Fifth Avenue, New York, NY 10010.

For more information, please visit www.kingfisherbooks.com

Printed in China
9 8 7 6 5 4 3 2 1
1TR/1014/WKT/UG/128MA

Note to readers: the website address listed above is correct at the time of going to print. However, due to the ever-changing nature of the Internet, website addresses and content can change. Websites can contain links that are unsuitable for children. The publisher cannot be held responsible for changes in website addresses or content, or for information obtained through a third party. We strongly advise that Internet searches should be supervised by an adult.

# CONTENTS

# Introduction
## Climate Change

When scientists study climate and weather, they look at energy and how it moves around the planet. Earth's energy comes from the Sun. Some of this energy is trapped by the planet, and some is reflected back into space. How much energy gets trapped (or reflected) is determined by the makeup of the air, as well as the amount of land, water, and ice on Earth's surface. Increased energy in Earth's atmosphere and its oceans changes the planet's weather patterns.

Earth has always had warmer and cooler periods. In the past, entire seas have dried out and ice ages have come and gone. This warming and cooling is natural—driven, for example, by predictable changes in Earth's orbit around the Sun. But scientists say that recent changes in Earth's climate have also been caused by human activity. Humans burn fossil fuels, which release carbon dioxide ($CO_2$) into the air. And a rise in $CO_2$ in the atmosphere causes warming. This is what is meant in this book by "climate change"—a warming of the planet caused by human activity in combination with natural forces. We need to discover ways of dealing with this human-driven climate change, so let's find out more.

Climate Change

# Chapter 1
## Global Gang

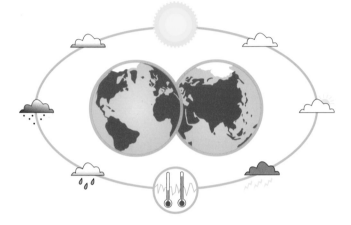

These guys are major movers and shakers when it comes to what happens on Earth. The Sun may be a staggering 93 million miles (150 million km) away, but this powerful source of energy has a big influence over our planet, as you are about to find out. Meanwhile, Ocean and Atmosphere soak up Sun's heat and shunt it around, making Climate and Weather change constantly. Other natural phenomena, such as El Niño and La Niña, affect Climate, too. You'll also meet Greenhouse Effect, whose trapping of Sun's heat is on the rise thanks to human activities. Let's find out what they have to say for themselves.

Sun

Atmosphere

Weather

Climate

Ocean

Glacier

Sea Ice

Carbon Cycle

El Niño

La Niña

Milankovitch Cycles

Greenhouse Effect

Ice Age

Snowball Earth

Climate Change

Global Dimming

# Sun
## Global Gang

☀ This dazzling ball of fire is the center of the solar system
☀ It is the closest star to Earth (93 million mi. or 150 million km away)
☀ The Sun's energy drives weather and long-term climate

Good day, sunshine! I'm a little sunbeam, a ray of light for the planet. Nuclear fusion reactions take place in my core and flood Earth with infrared, visible, and ultraviolet rays—those rays bring heat, light, and sunburn.

Every 11 years or so, raging magnetic storms on my surface boil over and then calm down again. I'm simply bursting with an energy that heats up the land, the air, and the oceans. But my heat doesn't spread evenly, and this means that I get Ocean circulating and stir up Atmosphere. All of this activity creates differences in pressure from one place to the next—differences that drive wild Weather. Obviously, I have a big effect on Climate, but the current rate of climate change is not all caused by me. Oh no, you humans have much to answer for there!

● Sun's surface temperature: 10,300 °F (5,700 °C)
● Time it takes for sunlight to reach Earth: 8.3 minutes
● World's sunniest city: Yuma, Arizona, with 4,000 hours of sunlight per year

# Sun

# Atmosphere
## ◼ Global Gang

✳ The thin layer of gases that wraps around Earth
✳ Mostly composed of nitrogen (78%) and oxygen (21%)
✳ Uses the weather to spread heat and water around

I wrap around Earth like a gas-filled comfort blanket, keeping the planet cozy and shielding life from a bombardment of lethal radiation from space. I'm made of nothing but air, but I'm no lightweight. In fact, you have a ton of air pressing down on you right now.

Some 63 percent of my bulk lies in the first 5 miles (8km) above the ground. Higher up, my gases become thinner and thinner. I have five gassy layers: weather thrashes around and jet liners fly in my lowest level, the troposphere, from the surface up to around 10.5 miles (17km); Ozone Layer lurks in my stratosphere,10.5–31 miles (17–50km); meteors crash and burn in my mesosphere, 31–53 miles (50–85km); space stations orbit in my thermosphere, 31–429 miles (85–690km). Then, at 455+ miles (700+km), my exosphere stretches halfway to the Moon!

● Official boundary of space: 62 mi. (100km) (Kármán Line)
● Mass of the atmosphere: 5.5 quadrillion (5,500,000,000,000,000) tons
● "Death zone": 5+ mi. (8km) where there is not enough oxygen in the air to survive

# Atmosphere

# Weather
## ■ Global Gang

❄ The state of Earth's atmosphere—hot or cold, calm or stormy
❄ Affected by the seasons, which are driven by the tilt of Earth
❄ Occurs in the troposphere level of the atmosphere

Forever on the move, I'm a Here Today, Gone Tomorrow kind of guy. It may be sunny today, but it won't be long before it rains. Hey, but the rain will stop once the storm passes. That's me, you see, ever changeable!

I'm prone to wild outbursts. Weather forecasters can make reasonable guesses as to my behavior over a week, but beyond that my chaotic nature leaves them clueless. As a rule, zones of high pressure are generally fair and dry, while low pressure brings out my nasty side —overcast skies, rain, and worse! Atmosphere's pressure differences create winds, and winds drive huge masses of air, called "fronts," around the planet. When these "fronts" collide, I come into my own! I'm not frontin' you—and Climate Change is just gonna make me wilder!

● Earth's typical temperature range: 40 to 104 °F (−40 to 40 °C)
● Most rain in a day: 71.9 in. (1,825mm) (Foc-Foc, Réunion, 1966)
● Largest hailstone: 18.7 in. (47.6cm) circumference (Aurora, Nevada, 2003)

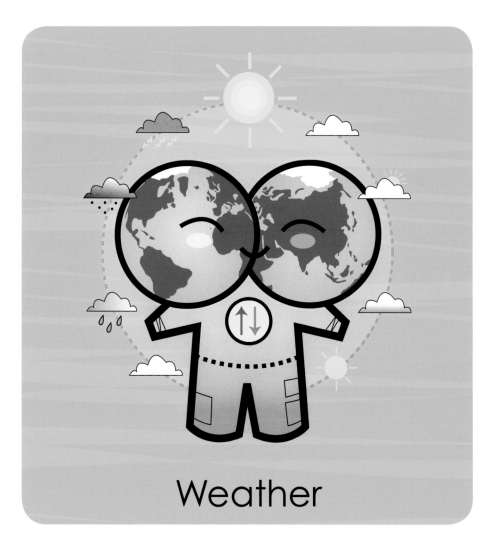

# Weather

# Climate
## ■ Global Gang

※ The "average" weather in a region
※ Depends on water availability and makeup of the atmosphere
※ Latitude and altitude play a role in climate, too

People tend to get me confused with Weather, but I'm nothing like that changeable dude. I'm solid and dependable—the kind you can always rely on. You see, Climate is what you expect; Weather is what you get.

Day-to-day weather is unpredictable, but over a number of years, a pattern starts to emerge, and that's where I come in. I am the typical weather a region has at a particular time of year—cool and wet in the spring, and hot and dry in the summer, for example. Places close to Earth's equator get a stronger blast of Sun's energy, so they tend to be hot. They may also be very dry (Sahara Desert) or very wet (Amazon rainforest). I like to change slowly, but over the past 100 years my changes have started speeding up. This will have effects for the whole planet and its people.

● Climate is normally measured over a period of 30 years or more
● World's wettest place: about 472 in. (12,000mm) rain/year (Khasi Hills, India)
● World's driest place: less than 0.004 in. (0.1mm) rain/year (Atacama Desert, Chile)

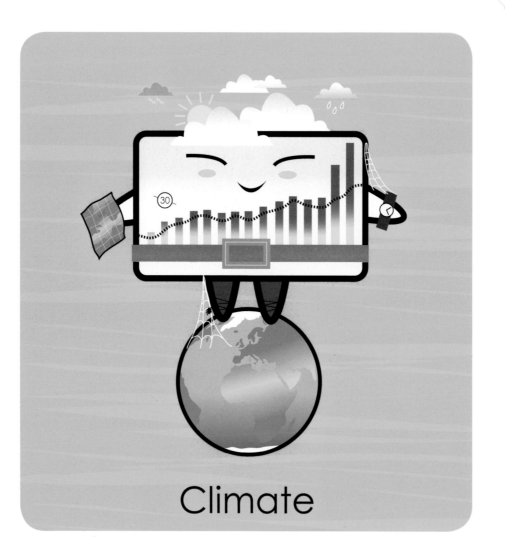

Climate

# Ocean
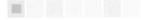

## ◼ Global Gang

✳ This watery bigwig covers more than two-thirds of Earth's surface
✳ Earth's five major oceans are all connected
✳ Part of the water cycle and acts as a carbon sink

I'm the planet's largest surface feature. I soak up Sun's rays and trap their heat—I hold more heat in my top 10 ft. (3m) than gassy Atmosphere can hold in its entirety. My pal Climate tends to be milder around me than inland. I absorb and release heat more slowly than land does, and this helps even out temperature extremes throughout the world.

My currents transport heat around the globe. They keep some places warmer and wetter than other places, even on the same latitude (think Gulf Stream and the British Isles). I'm also a huge bathtub for dissolving chemicals and gases—my waters are briny, thanks to the amount of salt dissolved in them. I suck up more than one-third of all carbon dioxide emissions made by humans, which makes me and Carbon Cycle pretty good buddies.

● The five major oceans are the Pacific, Atlantic, Indian, Southern, and Arctic
● Area of the world's oceans: 139 million sq. mi. (361 million km$^2$)
● Volume of water in the oceans: 312 million cu. mi. (1,300 million km$^3$)

Ocean

# Glacier
## ■ Global Gang

✳ Frozen, land-based ice formed by accumulation of snow
✳ Stable when accumulation exceeds loss through melting
✳ Climate change melts glaciers and raises sea levels

I am made of snow that fell faster than it could melt. I clothe Earth's polar and mountain regions in gleaming whiteness. Take care, though—it's a whiteness that can make you go "snow blind." In fact, I'm so reflective that I bring the planet's temperature down by beaming sunshine right back into space! It's an effect called "albedo"—Snowball Earth and Sea Ice can tell you more.

In some places (Greenland and Antarctica), I formed snowfall by snowfall over thousands of years. I preserve a record of the planet's past climate all locked up in my icy layers. Each year, I grow during the chilly winter months and melt in the summer. I also lose ice by calving, releasing big icebergs into the oceans. When Earth warms, I melt and sea levels rise. Drip, drip, drip . . .

● Includes mountain glaciers and polar ice sheets
● Size of Antarctic ice sheet: almost 5.4 million sq. mi. (14 million km$^2$)
● Size of Greenland (in the Arctic) ice sheet: about 656,000 sq. mi. (1.7 million km$^2$)

Glacier

# Sea Ice

## ■ Global Gang

☀ Frozen seawater that floats on the ocean
☀ Almost all of the Antarctic sea ice melts in the summer
☀ Helps keep the poles cold through reflective "albedo" effect

I'm super cool, and I'm not just talking chill factor. You see, water is one of the few substances that *expands* when it freezes (think cans of soda exploding in the freezer). It means that ice floats in water instead of sinking. Neat, huh?

I form when seawater freezes. Wind and ocean motion crack me into plates called ice floes, which jostle around in the water. I have a nasty habit of trapping and crushing ships that try to pick their way through gaps that open up between my floes. But don't confuse me with icebergs—Glacier can explain those. Polar bears hunt among my floes at the North Pole, and walrus rest on me between swims, but perhaps not for much longer. Each summer, a little more of me melts away. I don't raise sea levels like Glacier does, but the animals will miss me when I'm gone.

● Area covered by sea ice: about 10 million sq. mi. (25 million km²)
● Thickness of Antarctic sea ice: up to 3 ft (1m) thick
● Thickness of Arctic sea ice: up to 10–13 ft. (3–4m), with ridges 65 ft. (20m) thick

# Sea Ice

# Carbon Cycle
## Global Gang

* This cycle moves a key ingredient of life around the planet
* Earth's rocks are by far the biggest storehouses of carbon
* Human activity (burning fossil fuels) releases $CO_2$

I'm totally loopy. One of Earth's most important processes, I put carbon on an endless spin cycle. Mine is a complex, five-part program that involves living things, the soil, the air, the sea, and human activity.

The cycle starts when animals breathe out carbon dioxide ($CO_2$) and plants take it in. Plants use the $CO_2$ to build their bodies, and then animals eat the plants. When plants and animals die, carbon stored in their bodies gets locked into Earth as sediment. Over time, geological processes recycle this buried carbon, sometimes with volcanoes blowing enormous quantities of $CO_2$ into the air. Meanwhile, a lively and constant exchange of gases goes on between Atmosphere and Ocean. And then you humans go adding more $CO_2$ to Atmosphere . . .

● Typical volcanic eruption: 11 million tons $CO_2$ (Mount St. Helens, 1980)
● Human-related $CO_2$ emissions: 25 billion tons per year
● Human activity equates to around seven Mount St. Helens eruptions a day

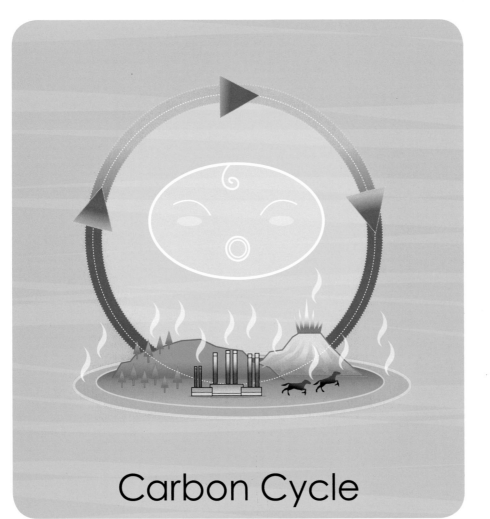

# Carbon Cycle

# El Niño
## ■ Global Gang

☀ Warm phase of the "Southern Oscillation" weather pattern
☀ Disrupts the normal circulation in the Pacific Ocean
☀ Occurs every two to seven years and lasts for about a year

A bringer of mixed fortunes, I usually show up around Christmas. Weakening normal east-to-west trade winds across the Pacific Ocean, I thrash the west coast of Peru and Ecuador with my storms and cause drought in Australia and Southeast Asia. When I am strong, I can cause extreme weather across the United States and might even affect Europe.

El Niño

● Southern Oscillation discovered: 1924 (Gilbert Walker)
● Most deadly El Niño: 1876–1877 (caused widespread famine)
● Average west Pacific sea level: 1.5 ft. (0.5m) higher than east Pacific sea level

# La Niña
## Global Gang

* Cool phase of the "Southern Oscillation"
* Blows stronger east-to-west winds across the Pacific Ocean
* La Niña means "girl" in Spanish; El Niño means "boy"

La Niña

I'm sometimes called the anti-El-Niño, but I prefer little girl! I almost always follow El Niño and have almost the opposite effect. While El Niño often reduces India's monsoon rains, I tend to swell them . . . and cause floods in Australia! Like El Niño, I am a "natural" weather pattern, and I boost the power of North Atlantic hurricanes. What a naughty girl!

* La Niña occurs every 3–6 years
* It can last up to 3 years
* Temperatures can drop by as much as 9 °F (5 °C) in the east Pacific Ocean

# Milankovitch Cycles

■ Global Gang

✳ Wobbles in Earth's orbit that cause changes in global climate
✳ Affects the amount of the Sun's radiation reaching Earth
✳ Changes which parts of Earth receive most energy from the Sun

Earth wobbles like a spinning top as it orbits Sun. These wobbles affect how much of Sun's radiation any part of the planet receives at any time, setting up my natural cycles of warming and cooling. My unsteady activity has the power to change the pattern of seasons, and even the entire global climate.

Here's what happens: the gravity of giant planets such as Jupiter and Saturn pulls on Earth and make its orbit go from a near-perfect circle around Sun to an eccentric ellipse. This wobble takes 100,000 years. The planet also bobs up and down on a 41,000-year timescale. Even the poles bob and wheel around, taking 26,000 years. And so it goes on!

● Current tilt of Earth: 23.5°; Variation in Earth's tilt: 22.1°–24.5°
● Calculation of long-term climate changes caused by changes in Earth's position: 1930s (Milutin Milankovitch)

Milankovitch Cycles

# Greenhouse Effect

## Global Gang

* Keeps our planet warm enough for life
* Caused by atmospheric gases that trap Earth's heat
* Satellites orbiting Earth measure the heat lost to space

I'm a hothouse flower. Without me, Earth's warmth would be lost to space every night, making the planet so cold that you'd have real trouble sleeping. No, sir, I keep Earth at a comfortable 59 °F (15 °C) instead of a glacial 0 °F (−18 °C).

I keep radiant energy from escaping from the planet. When Sun's glowing beams hit Earth, both land and sea absorb their energy. Earth heats up and radiates slightly less energy back into Atmosphere. Hanging out in multilayered Atmosphere are the members of the Greenhouse Gang (you'll meet them later). These guys have molecules that absorb the heat radiation coming from Earth. They act like an extra blanket, making Atmosphere super sweaty. Well, I won't tell you what happens next—I'll leave that to my pal Climate Change.

● Joseph Fourier figured out that the greenhouse effect warmed Earth (1820s)
● Amospheric $CO_2$ concentrations in 1850: 270 parts per million (ppm)
● Atmospheric $CO_2$ concentrations in 2014: 400 parts per million (ppm)

# Greenhouse Effect

# Ice Age

❄ Cold periods with permanent icecaps at Earth's poles
❄ Glacial periods are cold, with lots of glaciers and sea ice
❄ We are currently in a warmer "interglacial period" of an ice age

I am an icy blast. With help from that unsteady fellow, Milankovitch Cycles, I force chilly Glacier and Sea Ice to spread out from the polar regions. I blanket the land in snow and cover the sea in ice. Glaciers grow and spill down mountainsides, carving out valleys beneath them. To survive during the last ice age, many creatures grew thick, shaggy coats. Brrr!

Ice Age

● The late Cenozoic ice age started 2.58 million years ago
● Sea level during the last ice age: 400 ft. (120m) lower than current sea level
● Major ice ages in the history of the Earth: at least five

# Snowball Earth
## Global Gang

* The idea that planet Earth was once encased in slushy ice
* Attempts to explain ancient glacial activity in the tropics
* Thought to have been caused by a runaway albedo effect

Snowball Earth

Merely a scientific theory, I'm Ice Age gone crazy! The idea is that Glacier and Sea Ice pushed their way from the poles and extended to the equator. As the ice reflected more of Sun's energy away from Earth, the albedo effect increased, triggering an enormous cold snap. But then a warming period began, releasing greenhouse gases from volcanoes once again. Whew!

● First snowball Earth: 2.4–2.1 billion years ago
● Snowball Earth theory: 1992 (Joseph Kirschvink)
● $CO_2$ levels needed to break out of snowball: 13% (350 times today's levels)

# Climate Change

## Global Gang

* Earth's climate has changed over periods in the past
* The rate of change has increased over the past half century
* This recent change is the result of human activity

I'm a total hottie. Sure, I might sound cozy, but I spell trouble for the planet. Some say I'm a fairy tale—they wish! I'm real, all right. I'm right here, right now, and I'm going to bring major change.

No one knows exactly what will happen as Earth heats up, but one thing is for certain: a big thaw. Frozen water—say, Glacier—melting will cause flooding so that islands and low-lying areas will find themselves below the waves rather than above them. Ecosystems will change in polar regions and newly flooded zones. With less ice, less of Sun's energy will be reflected back into space, resulting in more warming and even more melting. Can humans stop this from happening? I can't tell you, but it sure is something to think about.

● Global temperature rise (1906–2005): 33 °F (0.56 °C)
● Longest continuous record of atmospheric $CO_2$ started at Mauna Loa, Hawaii: 1958 (Charles Keeling)

# Climate Change

# Global Dimming

## ■ Global Gang

✳ Prevents the Sun's full energy from reaching Earth's surface
✳ Has an overall cooling effect on the planet's temperature
✳ Smoke and pollution cause dimming

I'm one gloomy soul. Like a pair of shades for the planet, I cut out the glare when it's getting too bright. I'm an effect that happens when particles in Atmosphere block Sun's brightening rays when looking from Earth out to space.

I'm all about aerosols in the sky—tiny floating particles that are released when stuff is burned and volcanoes erupt. The particles cause a haze that blocks sunlight. They can also help clouds form, and we all know how clouds block out the light. Because I have a cooling effect, I counteract Climate Change. This makes people worry that I mask that hothead's true force. But I don't affect all parts of the world equally—China and India suffer more, while places with less pollution (Europe and the U.S.) are currently experiencing my opposite—global brightening!

● Term coined by Gerry Stanhill (1992)
● Dimming years: 1950s to 1990
● Brightening years: 1990 to present day

# Global Dimming

# Chapter 2
## Trackers 'n' Modelers

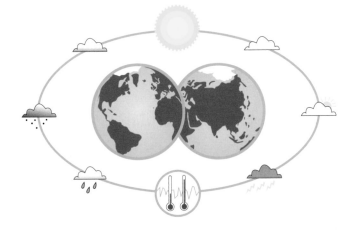

This slick team keeps a beady eye on Weather and Climate. Weather Station is based on land, offshore, and high in the sky, while Remote Sensing Satellite spins around the planet. The two of them collect raw data and feed it to the Modelers. The Modelers use supercomputers to crunch up-to-the-minute info and predict the future direction of the planet's climate. The marvelous Modelers and terrific Trackers help Climate Model make ever more accurate forecasts of changes in the climate. Meanwhile, smart Paleoclimate and Ice Core tell us about Earth's climates thousands or even millions of years ago.

Weather
Station

Remote Sensing
Satellite

Paleoclimate

Ice Core

Climate Model

Forcing
Mechanism

Positive
Feedback

Negative
Feedback

Tipping Point

Gaia
Theory

# Weather Station
## ■ Trackers 'n' Modelers

☀ Part of a global network used for weather forecasting
☀ Equipped with instruments that measure the atmosphere
☀ Includes weather buoys, balloons, and satellites

Bristling with ultrasensitive equipment, I'm the ultimate weather watcher. I monitor what happens out and about. Any changes I spot help scientists forecast future weather and keep track of long-term changes in Climate.

Boy, do I have some great instruments: a barometer for measuring atmospheric pressure; hygrometers for sensing water vapor in the air; an anemometer for wind speed; and a rain gauge for collecting and measuring rainfall. I get everywhere and go places that humans wouldn't dare! Loaded onto storm-watching weather balloons, I soar high up in the air to check up on Atmosphere. At sea level, I sit in buoys moored on anchoring cables or set adrift on Ocean's currents. My most high-tech version, fellow tracker Remote Sensing Satellite, is worth a look.

● First weather balloon: 1892 (Gustave Hermite and Georges Besançon)
● Typical weather balloon flight: 22 mi. (35km) up; 186 mi. (300km) drift; 2 hrs long
● Size of anchored buoy: 5–39 ft (1.5–12m) diameter

# Weather Station

# Remote Sensing Satellite

■ Trackers 'n' Modelers

✳ Space-based technology for observing Earth
✳ Relies on different wavelengths of visible and invisible light
✳ Watches over El Niño's tricks and monitors the ozone hole

Sometimes you need a little distance to see things more clearly, and that's where I come in. An all-seeing eye in the sky, I monitor the weather and land surface from on high. Wheeling around the planet, I have cameras for taking snaps of weather systems, cloud cover, and land use.

I am sensitive to emitted radiation given off by hot things. This means I can create heat maps that show ocean temperatures, currents, and eddies. This is how I keep my beady eye on El Niño. I can spy on city lights, forest fires, sandstorms, dust storms, desertification—you name it. I also like to keep my eye on Deforestation, Smog, Sea Ice, and poor, melting Glacier.

● Satellite altitudes: polar: 530 mi. (853km); geostationary: 22,300 mi. (35,888km)
● Time to orbit Earth: about 100 minutes (polar orbit)
● First weather satellite: 1960 (TIROS: Television and InfraRed Observation Satellite)

# Remote Sensing
# Satellite

# Paleoclimate
## Trackers 'n' Modelers

☀ The main climate for a period of time in the past
☀ Based on evidence found in rocks, plants, and corals
☀ Tiny sea animals hold records of ocean chemistry in their shells

I'm a dusty old record keeper that knows what the climate was like before you humans came along. But you've got to be smart to find me. Look at the growth rings of a tree and they will tell you something about the climate in that tree's past. Pollen trapped in mud and rocks tells you whether the plants living through an age were hot- or cold-climate types. That's all my work.

Paleoclimate

● Modern temperature records with instruments began about 1850
● Warming over past century: ten times faster than other warming episodes
● Event revealed through Paleoclimate: 1816 was a year without a summer

# Ice Core

## Trackers 'n' Modelers

※ A cylinder of ice drilled out from solid ice sheets and glaciers
※ Preserves a record of climates from the very distant past
※ Helps us understand the ways in which climate changes

Ice Core

I'm Paleoclimate's Popsicle pal, an ice-cool customer drilled out of the polar icecaps. I'm brought to the surface with a whoosh of escaping gas, like when you open a soft drink can. As snow falls year after year, the ice preserves traces of Atmosphere trapped inside. Superfine volcanic ash found within my layers can be linked with known eruptions to discover when I formed.

● Oldest temperature record from an ice core: 800,000 years
● Longest ice cores: 2 mi. (3km)
● Peak of last glacial maximum: about 20,000 years ago

# Climate Model

## ■ Trackers 'n' Modelers

✳ Climate models can help predict future climate changes
✳ They are run on supercomputers testing different scenarios
✳ Models agree that extra greenhouse gases cause warming

Look into my crystal ball and you'll see that I'm a high-tech fortuneteller for the world's future climate. And my predictions are way better than guesswork, believe me.

I collect up-to-the-minute data from my tracking pals, Weather Station and Remote Sensing Satellite, along with historical Paleoclimate know-how, and I use the info to make mathematical equations relating to the weather. Then I feed my equations into supercomputing systems. The better my equations match the real physics of Earth's systems, the more accurately I can predict the future (although some systems are simply too chaotic to be predictable). It's not all good news, I'm afraid: my work shows that the planet's rate of warming is increasing, and that means things could turn nasty.

● Number of lines of code in climate models: more than one million
● Time step: 30 minutes
● Total number of time steps in a typical 100-year model run: 1,753,152

# Climate Model

# Forcing Mechanism

■ Trackers 'n' Modelers

☀ Factors that "push" global temperatures up or down
☀ Can be "internal" (on Earth) or "external" (from outside Earth)
☀ The feedback twins boost or dampen its effects

I'm a pushy character—a real bossy pants! I work with the Feedback duo to shunt the temperature of the planet up ("positive forcing") or push it down ("negative forcing").

I meddle with the energy that Earth receives from Sun. Wobbles in Earth's orbit (Milankovitch Cycles) and Sun's natural cycle mean that the energy the planet receives can change. More or less of Sun's energy can reach the surface, too—for example, dust clouds from volcanoes block out light. Also, the energy reaching the surface might become trapped by greenhouse gases. Most forcing mechanisms are natural, but humans chip in by adding extra greenhouse gases.

● Total incoming solar radiation: 32 watts per sq. ft. (342W/m²)
● Period of solar cycle: 11 years on average
● Forcing due to greenhouse gases made by humans: 0.2 W/sq. ft. (2.3W/m²)

Forcing Mechanism

# Positive Feedback

■ Trackers 'n' Modelers

✳ Positive feedback boosts the effects of climate change
✳ Unlike forcings, feedbacks come from inside a climate system
✳ Water vapor resulting from warming causes more warming

I'm a chain reaction that feeds natural warming. As Earth's temperature rises, more of Ocean's water evaporates. Having more Water Vapor around means that more heat gets trapped in Atmosphere, making the world even hotter. Then Sea Ice melts, reflecting less light back into space, which results in greater heating. This slushy number is called the ice-albedo effect.

## Positive Feedback

● Amount of sunlight reflected by ice: 50–90%
● Amount of sunlight reflected by open water: 7%
● Larsen B ice shelf: 1,255 sq. mi. (3,250km²) lost in 3 weeks, 2002

# Negative Feedback

## Trackers 'n' Modelers

* Negative feedback dampens the effects of climate change
* Balance of forcings and feedbacks sets rate of climate change
* The hotter Earth gets, the faster it loses heat to space

Negative Feedback

While my positive pal reinforces Forcing Mechanism's effects, I can reduce them. Take those warming periods. I can slow down the rate of change and bring some much-needed cooling. With me around, all that evaporation of surface water makes more clouds. More clouds reflect more sunlight, thus bringing down the world's temperature.

- One of the important "dampening effects": clouds
- Amount of emitted $CO_2$ absorbed by ocean and land: 50%
- Lifetime of $CO_2$ in atmosphere: 30–90 years

# Tipping Point

## ■ Trackers 'n' Modelers

✳ A point at which a system changes—rapidly and substantially
✳ In the climate system, this could have global implications
✳ Gases from thawing permafrost could trigger global warming

I'm a character right on the edge, ready to flip at any time! And if I topple over, I'm likely to change from one state to another. I could take a lot of getting used to in my new form and, worse still, it could be a long time before I revert back to normal again.

Here is an example of something that could happen. The frozen peat bogs of western Siberia contain millions of tons of the powerful Greenhouse Gang member Methane. If a change in climate causes the permafrost to melt, the methane released will drive a new period of warming. Also, as the planet heats up, Ocean becomes less and less able to absorb fellow Greenhouse Gang member $CO_2$. The tipping point comes when Ocean switches from being a $CO_2$ absorber to a $CO_2$ producer.

● Amount of $CO_2$ humans add to the atmosphere: 25 billion tons per year
● World's largest peat bog: 400,000 sq. mi. (1 million km²) (western Siberia)
● Amount of Northern Hemisphere covered with permafrost: 25% (2013)

# Tipping Point

# Gaia Theory

✳ Theory that explains how life regulates the planet
✳ This good "mother" keeps Earth a suitable place for life
✳ Earth's systems seek to balance out changing conditions

*Yassou* (hello, in Greek)! I'm the good guardian. I'm named after the mother Earth goddess, and I've kept planet Earth just right for all living things for almost four billion years.

One of my main tasks is regulating temperature—too hot or too cold and life can't survive. Just look at the other planets of the solar system! Chemicals produced by life forms help maintain and protect Earth—check out the members of the Greenhouse Gang to see what I'm talking about. Earth has complex systems (you've already met Carbon Cycle). Each time one of these systems goes out of whack, the others help restore it. Milankovitch Cycles take the world out on a cooling path, but Earth hasn't frozen over for more than 650 million years. It's all a question of balance.

● Gaia theory: 1972 (James Lovelock)
● Oxygen first produced by life forms: about 2,500 million years ago
● Saltiness of the oceans: a steady 3.5%

Gaia Theory

# Chapter 3
## Greenhouse Gang

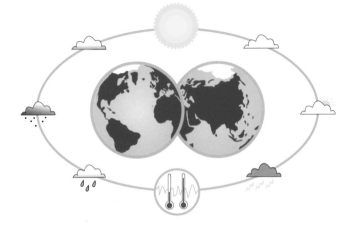

Meet the Greenhouse Gang, a bunch of global gases who play around with the planet's temperature. Global Gang member Atmosphere contains tiny amounts of these gases, but they have a big effect. Okay, so we can thank them for making the world a cozy place to live in, but let's not get carried away. These guys absorb long-wavelength infrared radiation coming off Earth's surface, and they trap the heat in gassy Atmosphere. Most members of this gang are entirely natural, but there's a fine balance—too much of them and the heat gets turned up. Better look out, too, 'cause they're on the rise!

# Sulfur Dioxide
## ■ Greenhouse Gang

✷ Sulfur dioxide is a powerful polluting gas
✷ A toxic scoundrel and a major cause of acid rain
✷ This polluting gas is released by burning petroleum products

I'm an unpleasant little devil, brimming with bad intent. You can't see me because I'm a colorless gas, but with a puff of smoke and a flick of my tail, I make a sharp and suffocating odor. (Think rotten eggs and burned matches!)

A nasty form of pollution, I wreak merry havoc with stuffy Atmosphere. I react with water to make acid rain, and I have a bad habit of forming choking blankets of Smog. Not a nice combo! Volcanoes and forest fires release me into the sky, but I am also pumped out by coal-burning power plants and by ships and train engines running on high-sulfur fuels. Luckily, I exist only in vanishingly small amounts and, these days, pollution-controlling devices called scrubbers help cut down on the amounts of me that get released by you humans.

● Chemical formula: $SO_2$
● Peak emissions: about 165 billion lb. (75 billion kg) (1980)
● Lifetime in the atmosphere: one to five days

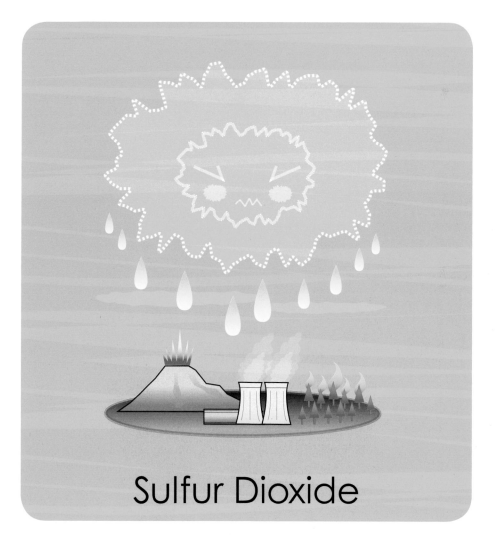

# Sulfur Dioxide

# Ozone

## ■ Greenhouse Gang

✶ The fifth-ranking greenhouse gas
✶ Pollutes at low altitudes while shielding Earth at high altitudes
✶ Ozone is a major ingredient of ugly urban smog

Made up of three oxygen atoms joined together, I am light blue as a gas, dark blue when liquid, and a deep violet-black when solid. I also happen to be a two-faced greenhouse gas . . . let me explain.

At ground level, I'm a real nuisance. Thanks to a chemical reaction powered by sunlight, I form irritating, throat-tickling Smog, polluted with hydrocarbons and nitrogen oxides. I am at least one thousand times better than gang member Carbon Dioxide at absorbing infrared rays emitted by Earth. Even so, I cause less damage because I don't stay around as long. High up in the stratosphere, I'm a superhero. About 6–30 miles (10–50km) up, a thin layer of me protects planet Earth from the worst of Sun's ultraviolet rays. See what I mean about two-faced?

● Chemical formula: $O_3$
● Percent by volume in air: 0.000004
● Lifetime in the atmosphere: 10 to 100 days

# Ozone

# Nitrous Oxide
## ■ Greenhouse Gang

✳ The fourth-ranking greenhouse gas
✳ A colorless, odorless gas with laugh-a-minute effects
✳ Several human activities contribute to $N_2O$ levels in the air

I'm a barrel of laughs! A whiff of my gas will make you giddy with laughter and will kill your pain in the dentist's chair. I may have some kick, but let me loose on old Atmosphere and it's no laughing matter.

Let's get a few things straight. I am a natural part of Earth's nitrogen cycle. In the sky, I'm a natural buffer keeping double-dealing Ozone under control. But with humans spreading fertilizers on fields, burning fossil fuels, and purifying water, my levels are slowly creeping up. This gives me a pretty fearsome rep as a member of the Greenhouse Gang, mainly because I tend to hang around long after the party's over. Pound for pound, I'm more than 300 times more powerful than Carbon Dioxide. I don't know whether to laugh or cry!

● Chemical formula: $N_2O$
● Percent by volume in air: 0.00003
● Lifetime in the atmosphere: 120 years

# Nitrous Oxide

# Methane
## ■ Greenhouse Gang

☀ The third-ranking greenhouse gas
☀ A gusty gas produced by animal burps
☀ $CH_4$ trapped in permafrost is a ticking time bomb if the ice melts

For the record, I'm *not* a big farty-pants. Stinky farts are made with the molecule methanethiol, which *looks* like me, but has an added sulfur atom ($CH_3SH$). No, I'm a natural gas—the "cream" off the top of oil wells. I burn with the blue flame you see on your camping stove. One way or another—in your furnace or in a power plant—I heat your home and provide you with electricity.

I leak out of rocks, I'm released from oil and gas wells, and I ooze from rotting waste in landfill. Cattle and sheep belch me out in vast quantities. Number three in the pecking order, I'm a heavy hitter—20 times more powerful than Carbon Dioxide. My problem is that I lack the staying power of $CO_2$. Having low levels and a short lifespan means that I'm easier to deal with.

● Chemical formula: $CH_4$
● Percent by volume in air: 0.00017
● Lifetime in the atmosphere: 12 years

# Methane

# Carbon Dioxide

## ■ Greenhouse Gang

☀ The second-ranking greenhouse gas
☀ Colorless, odorless, and mildly acidic
☀ The main culprit of climate change

I'm totally smokin'. Like Water Vapor, I'm part of the natural cycle known as Carbon Cycle. I keep carbon moving around the globe. I'm essential to living things— plants and algae take me in; you breathe me out—and my levels vary throughout the year with growing cycles.

I'm released naturally from oceans, volcanoes, and the breath of animals. Natural emissions outweigh emissions made by humans by 20 times or more, but humans do insist on pumping Atmosphere full of my molecules. I pour out of smokestacks and exhaust pipes when fossil fuels are burned. Meanwhile, Deforestation adds me to Atmosphere and reduces the number of plants using me up. I may be less powerful than Methane and Nitrous Oxide, but I have more impact because I hang around longer. Shudder!

● Chemical formula: $CO_2$
● Percent by volume in air: 0.0382
● Lifetime in the atmosphere: 50 to 200 years

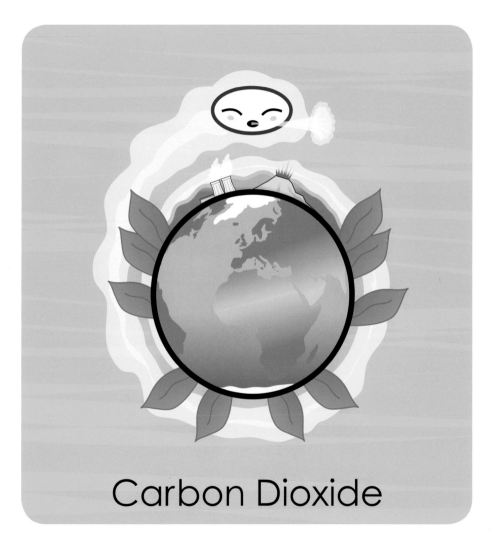

# Carbon Dioxide

# Water Vapor
## ■ Greenhouse Gang

✻ The top-ranking greenhouse gas
✻ The hotter air gets, the more water vapor it can hold
✻ $H_2O$ has the power to boost $CO_2$'s heating effect

I may be water, but I ain't wet. The kingpin of this gassy gang, I cause almost two-thirds of the greenhouse effect —natural *and* forced. You can't keep tabs on me. I come and go as I please, and I never hang around for long.

As part of the natural water cycle, I can slip between liquid water and my gassy state easily and quickly. Usually, I'm invisible in the air, but when the air cannot hold any more of me, I turn into tiny droplets of liquid water (think of your breath on a cold day). It's very hard to limit me because my levels are controlled by air temperature and are not affected directly by human activity. My ability to absorb infrared radiation is best seen in deserts that are sizzling by day but get cold quickly at night. There's very little water vapor in the air to trap the heat.

● Chemical formula: $H_2O$
● Percent by volume in air: 1 to 4
● Lifetime in the atmosphere: around 10 days

# Water Vapor

# Chapter 4
Blue-Sky Busters

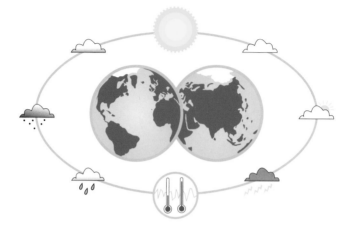

This group of highfliers fills the air around us. Swirling above our heads, the Blue-Sky Busters have the power to mess with the weather. They can make our cities miserable but also protect the planet from deadly radiation from outer space! Throat-blistering Smog and eye-watering Atmospheric Brown Cloud choke air close to the ground. Up high, meanwhile, ultrathin Ozone Layer has a gaping hole. Superfast Jet Stream drives weather fronts and is altering their predictable patterns in such dramatic ways that Frankenstorm could become a more frequent visitor. Yikes! Let's hear what they have to say . . .

Smog

Atmospheric Brown Cloud

Jet Stream

Ozone Layer

Frankenstorm

# Smog
## ■ Blue-Sky Busters

☀ This gritty urban character turns air into a nasty haze
☀ Caused by exhaust gases, dust, chemical sprays, and paints
☀ Harmful to health and can cause asthma or make it worse

I'm a flagon of foul air, a can of cough and splutter. A thoroughly unpleasant sandwich of the words "smoke" and "fog," I stick in the throat and make life miserable for city dwellers. I turn the air soupy with pollution, and when I get really nasty, I can burn your throat and eyes.

I exist in a haze of fine, almost invisible particles of soot, dust, and chemicals hanging in the air. In colder months, I'm caused mostly by people burning coal and wood to keep warm. In the summer, gases from burning fossil fuels combine in sunlight with chemicals called hydrocarbons to make a "photochemical" cloud, containing two-faced Greenhouse Gang member Ozone. Low-altitude Ozone is no fun. It's a reactive chemical that attacks plants and buildings, not to mention your delicate lungs!

● World's smoggiest cities: Ahvaz, Iran; Ulaanbaatar, Mongolia; Sanandaj, Iran
● Estimated deaths in Beijing, China, owing to smog: 2,589 (2012)
● Amount of coal burned in China: 4.2 billion tons (3.8 billion metric tons) per year

# Smog

# Atmospheric Brown Cloud

## ■ Blue-Sky Busters

☀ A blanket of pollution over large regions of the planet
☀ Has a global cooling effect on one hand . . .
☀ . . . but causes regional warming at the same time

I spread my dirty fingers across the sky. I sit like a giant brown stain over large areas of the world, such as East and South Asia. Scientists can see me from space!

I am mega Smog, caused by a mix of microscopic particles buoyed up in the air, having been released by coal-burning factories and power plants. I grow and become a deeper shade of brown when there is no rain to wash the particles out of the sky. I filter out sunlight, and scientists thought I might cause the world to cool, but I'm too sly for that. Particles of soot in my clouds absorb energy from Sun, boosting Atmosphere's heating effects. I pump out so much heat that I am rapidly melting glaciers in the Himalayas.

● First observed: 1999 (Indian Ocean Experiment)
● Height of atmospheric brown clouds (ABCs): 0.6–2.5 mi. (1–4km)
● Asian brown cloud: an ABC that appears over South and East Asia, Nov–May

# Atmospheric Brown Cloud

# Jet Stream
## Blue-Sky Busters

* Fast-flowing air currents high up in the atmosphere
* This jet setter steers mid-latitude storms around the globe
* Found in Earth's mid-latitude and subtropical regions

Start your engines, strap on your goggles, and come fly with me. I'm a daredevil speedster tearing along where the jet airplanes fly. My air currents snake around the planet like the ultimate pipe ride—a ribbon of fast-moving air that whizzes from west to east around the world in both the Northern and Southern hemispheres. Wheeee!

I am driven by temperature differences between the warm, muggy bodies of tropical air and cold, frigid masses of polar air. The pressure above rising masses of warm air at the tropics is higher than the pressure above falling polar air. This means that winds rush from low to high latitudes in order to equalize that pressure. The planet rotates at the same time, giving the air currents an eastward "kick."

● Jet-stream altitude: 4–7.5 mi. (6.4–12km) (polar); 6–10 mi. (9.6–16km) (subtropical)
● Top speed: more than 200 mph (322km/h)
● Discovery of the jet stream: 1920 (Wasaburo Oishi)

# Jet Stream

# Ozone Layer
## Blue-Sky Busters

* A thin layer of ozone ($O_3$) gas high in Earth's atmosphere
* A sunscreen layer for the planet, protecting against UV rays
* An ozone hole opens over Antarctica every year in the spring

Just like Greenhouse Gang member Ozone, I have a good side and a bad side. When I form close to Earth's surface, I'm a nasty polluting nuisance—the kind of stuff that makes throat-stinging, plant-killing photochemical Smog. But 12 to 17 miles (20 to 30km) above the surface, I'm a total blue-sky hero and a fully qualified lifesaver, to boot!

High up there, they call me "The Shield." I'm constantly produced and split apart, when incoming ultraviolet (UV) rays from Sun crash into Atmosphere. This absorbs almost all of the nasty "UVB" that gives you sunburn and is harmful to all living things. But there's bad news. I'm super thin, and chemicals called chlorofluorocarbons (CFCs) made by humans destroy me. This makes a great "hole" in the sky over Antarctica, where UV can sneak in after all.

● First discovered: 1913 (Charles Fabry & Henri Buisson)
● Concentration of ozone in stratosphere: 2–8 parts per million
● Discovery of ozone hole: 1985 (Farman, Gardiner, & Shanklin)

# Ozone Layer

# Frankenstorm

✷ An extreme storm that arises from a combination of factors
✷ A rise in seawater temperatures leads to fiercer hurricanes
✷ Climate change might cause more giant storm events

They call me the "perfect storm," but really I'm a monster —a raging, uncontrollable beast that brings destruction to everything within my reach. I'm totally extreme, and you'd better get used to me—meteorologists predict that you'll be seeing a lot more of me in the future.

In 2012, superstorm Sandy carved its way through the Caribbean Sea, ripping through everything in its path before reaching America, where it tore up 24 states. Savage Sandy caused so much mayhem that it was the most costly storm ever. As Climate Change makes Ocean's temperature rise, the air above the water grows increasingly warmer. And the warmer the temperature of Ocean becomes, the stronger the storm when it rages. You'd better run for cover!

● Hurricane Sandy 2012: Category 3 storm
● Diameter of storm: 1,100 mi. (1,800km)
● Sea temperatures off U.S. East Coast: 5 °F (3 °C) warmer than usual

# Frankenstorm

# Chapter 5
## Ocean Wavers

Discount the Ocean Wavers at your peril! Earth's enormous bodies of big blue absorb gazillions of tons of carbon dioxide and are the biggest sink for greenhouse gases. They retain heat much better than land does, so they help smooth out temperature extremes, making summers milder and winters less harsh. But all is not well. The oceans are rising as the planet gets warmer and more ice melts. Increasing $CO_2$ levels are making the water more acidic. And as the water temperature rises, storms that develop over tropical waters are becoming more severe. Looks like the Ocean Wavers are gonna make a splash!

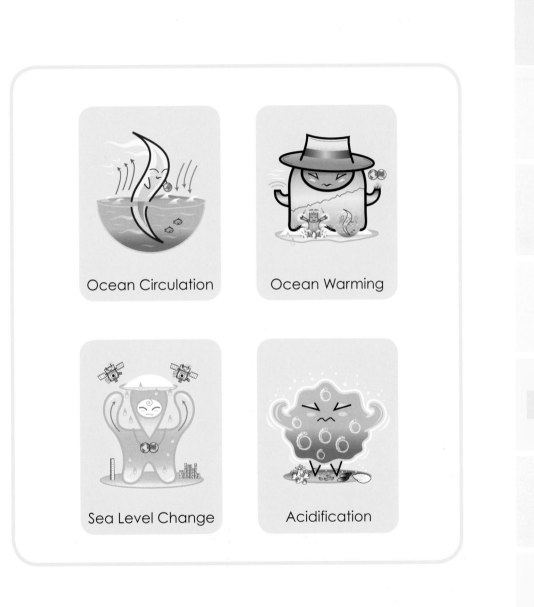

Ocean Circulation

Ocean Warming

Sea Level Change

Acidification

# Ocean Circulation
## Ocean Wavers

✳ The mechanism by which the oceans mix themselves
✳ Driven by wind and density (temperature/salinity) differences
✳ The movement of heat around the planet affects climate

I like to stir things, whipping up Ocean's water and transporting heat and nutrients around the globe. I'm driven by winds at my surface and temperature/salinity for my deep underwater currents.

Atmosphere's air currents (or surface winds) push Ocean's top 165 to 330 feet (50 to 200m) around. These swift-moving, mostly shallow currents include the Gulf Stream, which moves warm water from the Caribbean across the North Atlantic, keeping northern Europe warm and wet in the winter. Temperature differences between equatorial and polar waters, as well as variations in seawater saltiness, drive currents that go much deeper. As Climate Change boosts Ocean's heat—melting poor Glacier—my deep currents will start to run more slowly and may starve ocean life of vital nutrients.

● Largest ocean current: 125 Sv (Sverdrup), (Antarctic Circumpolar Current)
● Ocean current speed: 0.4 in.(1cm)/sec. (thermohaline); 39 in.(99cm)/sec. (wind)
● Time it takes for seawater to travel all around the globe: 1,000 years

# Ocean Circulation

# Ocean Warming
## ▪ Ocean Wavers

✳ An increase in the energy of the oceans
✳ The result of climate change, which mostly affects oceans
✳ Warmer water gives off more $CO_2$ than cooler water does

I am a global gangster, a dark and murky player behind the scenes. I pull the strings on Climate Change's game and turn up the heat on the planet. Sure, it makes for more pleasant swimming, but as the world warms up, poor Ocean is in danger of losing his cool.

I'm a much steadier type than Atmosphere, who absorbs and loses heat quickly. No, my temperatures are slow to change, and this makes me much more powerful. I hold on to my energy and use Ocean Circulation to move it around the globe. In warmer waters, polar ice caps will melt, leading to higher sea levels. I drive stronger, more frequent storms (think Frankenstorm), I alter Ocean's ecosystems, and I threaten food chains. I might even add to Atmosphere's heady Greenhouse Gang. Hot stuff, indeed!

● Rise of sea surface temperatures in 20th century: 0.13 °F (0.07 °C) per decade
● Estimated reduction in fish catches by 2050: 50%
● Amount of oxygen provided by marine plankton: about 50%

# Ocean Warming

# Sea Level Change
## Ocean Wavers

✷ This prankster floods low-lying areas of the planet
✷ Sea levels are expected to continue to rise for centuries
✷ Measured by remote sensing satellites (since 1992)

Pull on those rubber boots—it's going to get wet! I'm a soggy so-and-so whose main joy in life is spreading mayhem and misery. And because more than half the world lives within 37 miles (60km) of the seashore, there's more to my destructive work than wet feet.

Thanks to Climate Change, I'm on the way up! This is because water expands when the temperature rises. And when water expands, it takes up more space. Glacier melts, pouring even more liquid into sopping Ocean. As the water level goes up, cities go down. Low-lying areas, such as the Mississippi Delta in the United States and the Ganges Delta in Bangladesh, could flood, affecting millions of people. Long-term, the Italian city of Venice and the Maldives could disappear under the waves for good.

● Projected sea-level rise: 3 ft. (1m) by 2100
● Sea level during the Ice Age: 400 ft. (120m) lower than today
● Most at-risk islands: Maldives, Marshall Islands, Torres Strait Islands, Tuvalu, Nauru

# Sea Level Change

# Acidification
## Ocean Wavers

✻ Oceans are a sink (large storehouse) for carbon dioxide
✻ This fearsome fizzer is the result of raised levels of $CO_2$
✻ Acidification threatens shelled animals and coral reefs

I cut to the bone. I am a bitter and twisted side effect of an increase in $CO_2$ in Ocean. The Blue-Sky Busters and the Ocean Wavers constantly swap and share what they have. Where the sky meets the sea, gases in the air mingle and mix, dissolving easily into the water. So when Atmosphere's carbon dioxide levels go up, so do Ocean's.

More $CO_2$ in seawater makes it more acidic. Many sea creatures—such as coral, mollusks (squids and seashells), crustaceans (crabs and lobsters), echinoderms (starfish and sand dollars) and tiny plankton—build shells out of a hard mineral called calcium carbonate to protect their bodies. Extra acidity makes it harder to extract this mineral from the water and can even start to dissolve the shells of these critters. Coral reefs suffer badly, turning ghostly white and dying off.

● Human-made $CO_2$ absorbed by oceans: 26% per year
● Acidity increase in oceans: 100 times faster than any time in 20 million years
● Rate of coral reef death: twice as fast as rainforest loss

# Acidification

# Chapter 6
## Human Crew

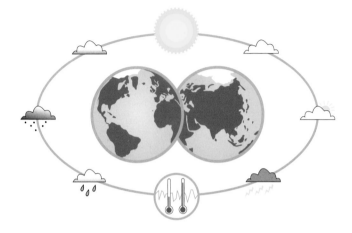

The Human Crew have a pretty bad rep. Relating to the activities of rich and industrialized nations, these guys have been cranking up pressure on the planet for more than half a century. Perhaps they just didn't think about the consequences? Well, Climate Change affects all living things—Fossil Fuel and Population Growth can tell you all about it. Thankfully, the facts are out about these dudes, and real efforts are being made to reduce their impact. You can make a difference, too—we all can. So find out what these guys have to say and then start taking care of this planet. After all, it's the only one we have!

# Fossil Fuel
■ Human Crew

※ Natural energy sources that are burned to generate electricity
※ They are made from things that lived millions of years ago
※ Living things are built of carbon; burning them releases $CO_2$

Made from the bodies of long-dead plants and animals, I lurk underground as coal, oil, and natural gas, just waiting to be dug up and burned. Compared with other fuels, I am chock-full of energy, and there's a lot of me around. I offer a pretty cheap way of making electricity. I just happen to be dirty.

The fumes that I produce when I burn create Smog and Atmospheric Brown Cloud. Carbon inside the dead bodies of plants and animals combines with oxygen to make carbon dioxide, and increased $CO_2$ causes Climate Change. People burn me to keep warm, to drive their cars, to power their electrical goods, and to manufacture products. Your food and merchandise travel to reach you, adding dirty carbon miles to many things you buy. It's time to start thinking about how to use less of me.

● $CO_2$ released per person in the U.S.: about 20 tons (18 metric tons) per year
● Amount of coal burned to create electricity: 80%
● Solar power is becoming as cheap as fossil fuels in some places

Fossil Fuel

# Deforestation

## ■ Human Crew

※ This slash-and-burn merchant cuts down forests
※ Rainforests in South America, Africa, and Southeast Asia suffer
※ Plants are awesome at absorbing carbon dioxide

I'm no ordinary lumberjack—I don't take care of forests, but destroy them for good. I'm a slasher. I slice down the woods, burn the trees, and lay good land to waste. I *love* to rev up the chainsaws and let the bulldozers roar!

I make way for human activity—both agricultural (cash crops and cattle ranches) and urban (building boom-time cities). Illegal logging for timber threatens native forests, and at the current rates of chopping I could strip the planet bare in 100 years. By taking away their habitat, I make it hard for woodland plants and animals to survive. Without trees drawing water out of the ground and releasing Water Vapor, land can quickly become dry and barren. When it rains, the parched soil washes away. And without plants to absorb $CO_2$, Climate Change just gets worse.

● Area of forest lost per year: 18 million acres (7.3 million hectares) (size of Panama)
● Amount of $CO_2$ added to the atmosphere through deforestation: 20%
● Proportion of world's land still covered by forests: 30%

# Deforestation

# Heat Wave
■ Human Crew

✸ Changing weather patterns caused by climate change
✸ Heat waves cause discomfort, death, drought, and forest fires
✸ Climate change could cause extreme weather of all kinds

I'm a mischievous type who just loves to meddle and mess with Weather. Crinkling up my leathery, over-tanned face, I'm turning up the heat and changing the planet's weather patterns for good.

You may love the idea of hotter weather—of being able to wear less and hang out at the beach. But excess heat stresses the human body and can prove fatal. Extended dry spells make crops fail, causing famine, while dried-out forests and brushwood are ready to blaze at the slightest spark. Scientists call me a "loaded dice"—that is, not every throw is a six (a hot summer), but over time there will be more hot summers than are normal. Some say this is a superstition, that they remember hotter times. Well, that may be, but those record highs just keep on coming.

● First use of term "heat wave": 1892 (New York City)
● Definition: when max temperature is 9 °F (5 °C) above average for 5 days running
● August 2003 European heat wave death toll: 70,000

# Heat Wave

# Population Growth
## ■ Human Crew

☀ The number of new people living on the planet every year
☀ An increase cranks up the pressure on the world's resources
☀ Cleaner green tech is needed to avoid severe climate change

People keep on having babies. And with improved health care, people live longer. All of this means that, year after year, I grow. More people need more land and more food. They use more energy and create more waste. As developing countries become richer and more industrial, the amount of Fossil Fuel burned by each person will boom. I see trouble ahead.

Population Growth

● World population growth: about 80 million people per year
● Total projected world population: 8–9 billion by 2040
● Time when world population will stop growing: 2050

# Urbanization
## Human Crew ■

- ☀ Today, half of the world's population lives in cities
- ☀ Urban population will increase as global population grows
- ☀ Cities create problems of landfill, smog, and $CO_2$ emissions

Urbanization

As Population Growth adds more people to the planet, I make the world's cities more crowded. All too often this means people live in poverty in unsafe, unhealthy slums. Booming population leads to environmental problems of mounting waste, dirty industries, and increased traffic. To avoid harsh, planet-altering Climate Change, it's time to look for solutions now!

- ● Total world population: 7.2 billion
- ● Population living in cities: 3.5 billion
- ● People living in slums: 1.5 billion

# Biological Systems
## ■ Human Crew

☀ Earth is a dynamic planet and reacts to changes
☀ Plants and animals migrate in response to changing climate
☀ Drought and crop failure may become more regular events

I'm Mother Nature, and I don't wait around. Threaten me, buster, and I take action! As weather systems change, storms swirl, and summers get hotter, I start to react. Seasons are shifting, and living things are on the move.

The growing season is gradually altering, making some areas unsuitable for certain crops. As the polar regions warm up, animals are moving in, heading for the poles. Those that prefer it cold are having to move away to find the climate and food they like. Species that have a limited range or a special diet, such as seals, walrus, and polar bears that rely on Sea Ice to survive, are running out of luck. As Ocean absorbs more Carbon Dioxide and becomes more acidic, sea life will suffer. And humans? They just can't keep up with my changes to the natural world!

● Northward shift of butterflies: 125 mi. (200km) (Europe and North America)
● Magellanic penguin chicks killed by global warming: 7% per year
● Area of Canadian forest affected by pine beetle infestation: 52,000 sq. mi.

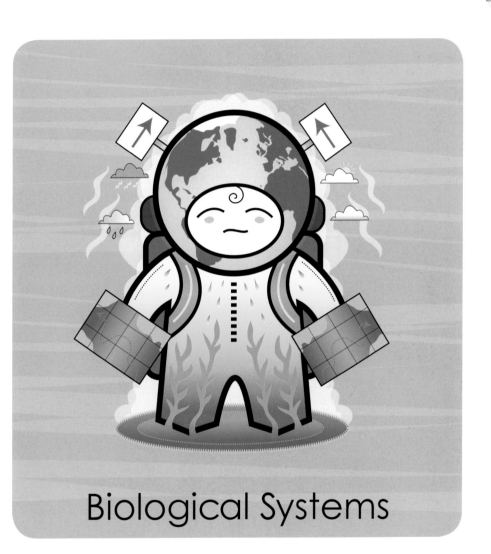

# Biological Systems

# Chapter 7
## Green Gang

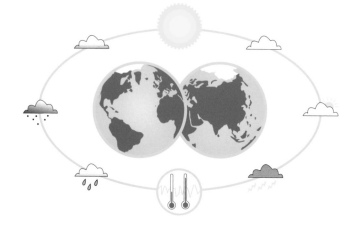

Enough talk—it's time for action! Here come the superheroes. With their "can-do" mentality, these guys don't spend time worrying and wringing their hands. They get right to work! Talk to Carbon Footprint and you'll get the idea. Sure, it takes energy from burning Fossil Fuel to establish and maintain some of the Green Gang members, but once up and running, their benefits really start to kick in. With dudes like Renewable Energy, Biofuel, and Nuclear Power around, the ultimate aim is to create "sustainable energy," where the energy we use doesn't warm the planet. Let's find out how they operate.

Carbon
Footprint

Carbon
Trading

Recycling

Renewable
Energy

Biofuel

Nuclear
Power

Green
Technology

Geo-
engineering

Carbon Capture
and Storage

Resurrection
Biology

# Carbon Footprint
## Green Gang

☀ Calculates the amount of $CO_2$ coughed into the air
☀ Fossil fuels are burned to make and shift goods, emitting $CO_2$
☀ Every person has their own carbon footprint

I am the carbon accountant. Fussy and fastidious, I total up all the carbon dioxide that a person, object, company, or country emits. I read the emissions as footprints.

The larger the footprint, the more damage it does to the environment. A lot of your food, clothes, and electronic goods come from countries far away. Getting them to you requires transportation—ships, aircraft, trucks, and trains—all burning Fossil Fuel. It takes energy to store, dispose of, and recycle these products, too. And you personally? Well, the fossil fuels burned when you travel or take a shower or watch TV—they all go into my ledger. But no excuses, now! There are plenty of ways to reduce your own footprint. You can walk to school instead of going by car, and buy food locally. Hey, and find a good book to read!

● Carbon footprint of apple from your backyard: 0lb. (0kg)
● Carbon footprint of a pair of jeans: 24 lb. (11kg)
● Carbon footprint of average person: 3.6 tons (3.3 metric tons)

# Carbon Footprint

# Carbon Trading
## Green Gang

✳ The trade of $CO_2$ emissions, controlled by the United Nations
✳ Reducing pollution in a way that allows people to make money
✳ Agreed in the Kyoto Protocol (1997), now signed by 192 nations

I'm Cap'n Trade, setting a course to reduce global $CO_2$ emissions. Some people dislike my methods, but at least I'm rolling up my sleeves and *getting things done!* I want to sail toward a brighter future. Let me tell you how.

First, I set a limit on the volume of carbon dioxide that industries can produce. Anyone who produces less than their allowance can trade their spare units with those who produce more. It's a kind of "swapsies" market for dirty pollution. Some say my system rewards polluters, because those who pollute more get more units. They say that making money out of pollution is wrong. But I say we have to start somewhere. Otherwise, industries won't even think about the greenhouse gases that they are pumping out—and that's bad for everyone!

● Carbon trading units: 1.1 ton (1 metric ton) "blocks" of $CO_2$
● Carbon emission trading AKA: "cap and trade"
● $CO_2$ emissions accounted for by signatories of Kyoto Protocol: at least 61%

# Carbon Trading

# Recycling
## Green Gang

✳ Conserving Earth's precious resources by reducing waste
✳ Household waste buried in the ground releases methane gas
✳ Organized collections gather up recyclables and biomass

What is it with you people and new stuff? Don't you get it? Buying new stuff uses up the limited quantities of raw materials on Earth. A whole lot of the energy used to make new products and ship them around the world comes from burning Fossil Fuel.

I say use less. Next time you need something, ask whether you *really* need it. And if you do, buy it secondhand. I love turning old stuff into new. Many materials, such as glass, metal, and plastic, can be used again and again. Sure, it takes energy to recycle products, but it often takes less energy than making a new product. Recycling aluminum takes five percent of the energy needed to extract and make new aluminum. So think about what you're about to throw away, and recycle it instead.

● Amount of $CO_2$ saved per ton (0.9 metric tons) of recycled glass: 371 lb. (168kg)
● Amount of electronic waste disposed: about 50 million tons per year
● 1 million cell phones gives: 35,000 lb. (15,875kg) copper; 75 lb. (34kg) gold

# Recycling

# Renewable Energy
## Green Gang

* Solar, wind, tidal, geothermal, and biofuel power
* Using renewable energy does not produce $CO_2$ pollution
* Renewable energy is the fastest-growing power source

I'm a bright spark, a ray of hope for a world choking on fumes from burning Fossil Fuel. Wake up, people! It isn't enough just to use energy-efficient light bulbs and drive a little less. It's time to change power sources.

I harness energy from sources that are always available. Solar power uses panels to collect Sun's energy and to heat water in pipes. Photoelectric cells can directly convert Sun's rays into electricity. Geothermal power uses the heat under our feet to make steam for driving turbines. Wind turbines use the power of blustery days to whirl propellers around to generate electricity, while hydroelectric power—the number one renewable— uses running water to do the same. What's the best thing about me? That's right, I produce not a whiff of Carbon Dioxide—I'm the clean dream.

● Global fossil fuel usage: 72%
● Global renewables usage: 17%
● Total heat loss from Earth: 4.42 trillion watts

# Renewable Energy

# Biofuel
## Green Gang

* Renewable energy that uses living matter to generate power
* Oily or sugar-rich plants are grown to make biofuels
* Biomass is one of the largest sources of renewable energy

I'm the green garbage man. Fossil Fuel is made from the remnants of living things pressed and juiced underground over millions of years. I say, why wait? I use organic matter, called biomass, available right here, right now.

I love household waste. Rotting garbage, crop cuttings, and human waste all release Methane. Instead of letting this landfill gas add to the greenhouse problem, I collect it as biogas. Other crops, such as sugarcane and corn, are grown especially to make a version of me that buses and cars can run on. Ten points if you guessed that producing and then burning me releases Carbon Dioxide. However, unlike Fossil Fuel, I'm not releasing $CO_2$ that's been locked up for eons. Plus, planting new vegetation sucks it back up. Vroom, vroom—let's burn green stuff!

● Total global biofuel production: 28 billion gal. (105 billion L)
● Typical biomass yield: 3.4–3.6 tons per acre (7.5–8 metric tons per hectare)
● Amount of carbon in dry wood: 50% by weight

# Biofuel

# Nuclear Power
## Green Gang

* Converts the energy stored in the nuclei of atoms
* Produces more energy per ton than any other fuel source
* A non-carbon-based energy source that doesn't produce $CO_2$

I'm Atomic Boy. I unleash the power locked inside the very heart of matter. Splitting apart atoms by the process of nuclear fission, I release torrents of energy!

I don't use materials that contain carbon—my reactors run on the heavy metal uranium. This means that I make cheap, plentiful, and clean energy. Many people hold me up as the savior of the planet. There's just *one* thing . . . You see, I create ultradangerous radioactive waste that takes ages to become safe. This stores up trouble for the future. Also, nuclear power plants are at risk from natural disaster, malfunction, or meltdown, which could release radioactive substances into nature. Nuclear accidents—like the one at Fukushima Daiichi, Japan, in 2011—can have terrible consequences. It's something I take very seriously.

- Energy density of uranium-235: 10.5 million kWh/lb. (83.1 million MJ/kg)
- Energy density of coal: 3 kWh/lb. (24 MJ/kg)
- Number of evacuees during Fukushima Daiichi disaster: 100,000

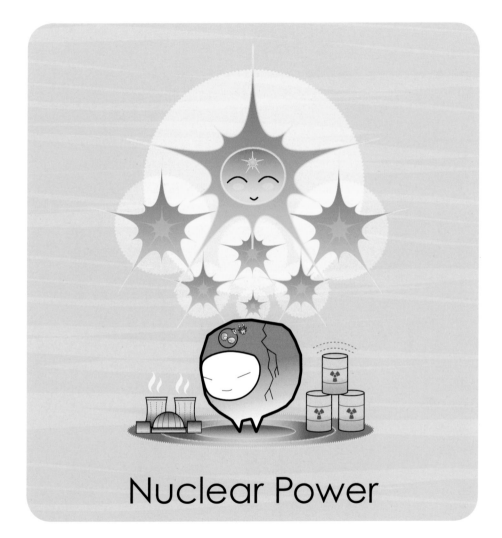

# Nuclear Power

# Green Technology

✳ Smart new technology that uses radically less energy
✳ Aims to reduce people's energy use by one-third by 2050
✳ Creative inventions for industry, transport, and domestic use

I'm a revolutionary, an inventor churning out novel ways to save energy and cut down on $CO_2$ emissions. If you want creative solutions, I'm way ahead of the game!

I believe in a world where everyone has access to technology, but for this to happen, those using the most energy have to cut down. Some of my ideas are totally high-tech—"smart" buildings, new household appliances using a fraction of the energy of older ones, and fuel cell batteries that can power a new generation of nonpolluting electric vehicles. Other ideas of mine are more oldschool—using bicycles for short trips and clotheslines to dry laundry, and turning off TVs and computers instead of leaving them on standby. See—you, too, can help save the planet.

● Tallest energy-efficient building in the U.S. (2011): Empire State Building
● Compact fluorescent lights (CFLs) use 75% less energy than incandescent bulbs
● LED lights use 84% less energy than incandescent bulbs

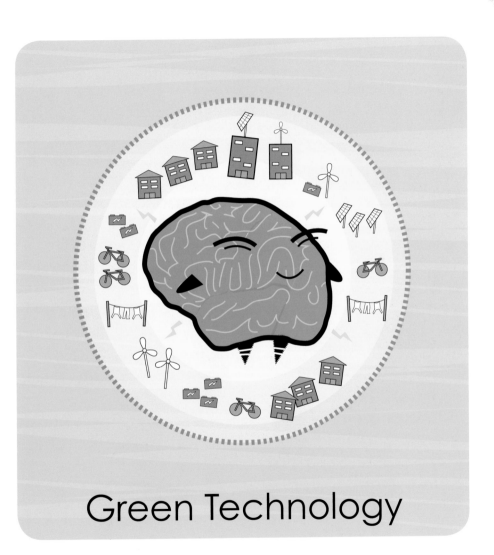

# Green Technology

# Geoengineering

## Green Gang

* Plans to stop and even reverse climate change
* Requires greater knowledge of how Earth's systems work
* No such attempts have ever been made before

Bold and ambitious, I am a schemer and a dreamer. My master plan is to alter the whole planet to stop Climate Change in its tracks, and I propose two lines of attack.

The first is to bring down Carbon Dioxide levels. The second is to reduce the amount of sunlight reaching Earth. I can use carbon storage to tuck $CO_2$ away in nooks and crannies. Feeding Ocean with iron would cause a bloom in photosynthesizing plankton microbugs, which suck up carbon dioxide as they grow. Space mirrors—giant reflective sails in orbit around Earth—would bounce away sunlight, while sulfate dust injected into Atmosphere could mimic the cooling effects of volcanoes. But these harebrained notions are extreme, and their side effects could be worse than the problems they are trying to solve!

● Total area of space mirror required: 1.5 million sq. mi. (3.8 million km²)
● Altitude of dimming sulfate aerosol injection: 7–10.5 mi. (11–17km)
● Amount of $CO_2$ fixed by 1 lb. (454g) of iron: 83,000 lb. (38,000kg)

Geoengineering

# Carbon Capture and Storage

✹ Capturing $CO_2$ and burying it where it can't cause harm
✹ Power plants are starting to bury carbon-waste gases
✹ Some think that burying $CO_2$ is like burying heads in the sand

I collect up the nasty stuff emitted by burning Fossil Fuel and bury it. This happens naturally when sea organisms absorb Carbon Dioxide from seawater and later die. They sink to the bottom of the ocean, turn into sediment, and lock carbon away forever inside rocks. I speed up the process.

I catch Carbon Dioxide—normally from industrial plants and transport it to a storage site through pipelines. Then I bury it underground in old coal mines, squirt it into wells to force the dregs out of an oil field, or react the gas with minerals to make new carbon-containing minerals. Storing $CO_2$ under the ocean is a no-no, because it makes seawater more acidic and it could erupt to the surface in a toxic "burp." Yuck!

● $CO_2$ produced by power plants that could be locked away: 80–90%
● Amount of $CO_2$ injected into U.S. oil fields: 30–50 million tons
● Potential area of CCS rock formations in U.S.: 6,200 sq. mi. (16,000km²)

# Carbon Capture
# and Storage

# Resurrection Biology

## Green Gang

- Genetic tech that could bring creatures back from extinction
- Only intact DNA from recent extinct animals can be used
- Technology could be used to help preserve threatened species

I'm a Genetic Wizard that can bring animals back from extinction. This may seem to go against nature, but it's a way we can mend the damage caused by Climate Change.

I employ the techniques used to clone Dolly the sheep in 1996. Genetic scientists inject an egg cell with the nucleus of an adult cell. It is "activated" and grown in the lab before being implanted into an animal mom, who gives birth to the new beast. Museums are storehouses of DNA, found inside bone and teeth fragments. I don't have the trick right yet, but the Pyrenean ibex is the top candidate to go first. Exciting stuff for sure, but we must first learn to take care of our existing species.

- First attempt: 2003 (Pyrenean ibex); attempt failed
- Number of ibex embryos reconstructed: 285
- Second attempt: 2009 ("de-extinct" ibex clone died after seven minutes)

# Resurrection Biology

# Index

# Glossary

**Acid rain** Rainfall that is made slightly acidic when water combines with sulfur dioxide and nitrogen oxide pollution in the air. It is harmful to plant life and things living in water.

**Albedo** The amount of the Sun's energy that is reflected directly back into space.

**Algae** Simple plants that do not produce flowers. Many of the single-celled plankton floating in the oceans are algae. Algae absorb energy from the Sun and carbon dioxide and release oxygen.

**Altitude** Height above Earth's surface.

**Bacteria** Single-celled microorganisms that are neither plants nor animals. Most living things on Earth are bacteria.

**Biomass** Material that comes from living things—trees, crops, grasses, household and animal waste—that can be burned to produce energy.

**Biosphere** All of the ecosystems and the organisms that live in them, incuding in the air, on land, and in the oceans.

**Cash crop** A crop that is grown to sell rather than for eating or using by the grower.

**Clone** A living thing or living cells that are exact genetic copies of their parents.

**Conduction** The way in which energy (heat) passes from hot to cold regions by making microscopic parts of a substance vibrate.

**Ecosystem** A system made of living things interacting with one another and their environment.

**Ellipse** An oval shape, like a squashed circle.

**Extinction** The process of a group of living things dying out and ceasing to exist on Earth.

**Hemisphere** Half of a solid sphere; the northern or southern half of the planet.

**Industrialize** The process by which a country becomes more industrial, by building more factories and power plants.

**Latitude** The distance away from the equator—north or south—measured in degrees (the angle between a place and the equator).

**Meteorologist** A scientist who studies the atmosphere.

**Migrate** When animals, such as birds, fish, and insects, move from one region or habitat to another with the change of seasons.

**Nuclear Fusion** Term used to describe the process of nuclear reaction when two or more atomic nuclei bind together, making a new nucleus of a heavier element and releasing energy in the process.

**Nutrients** The foods and substances that are essential for life and growth.

**Oscillation** A wobble or change of state that occurs at a regular speed. Climate oscillation involves changes in air, ocean temperature, and rainfall that drive a change in the weather pattern.

# Glossary

**Pack ice** Large pieces of floating ice that are joined together in one mass; found in polar seas.

**Permafrost** A thick layer of soil that remains frozen throughout the year.

**Quadrillion** 1,000,000,000,000,000 (one thousand trillion).

**Radiant energy** The energy of electromagnetic radiation that can travel across space. Energy reaching Earth from the Sun arrives in this form; Earth absorbs this energy and re-radiates a part of it back into space.

**Salts** Dissolved compounds in water that can make it taste salty. They are deposited as minerals when the water evaporates.

**Sink** Anything that acts as a storehouse for a substance; the oceans are sinks of carbon dioxide and heat because they absorb vast amounts of both.

**Troposphere** The lowest layer of the atmosphere, stretching from Earth's surface to about 4–6 mi. (6–10km) up. This is where weather occurs.